Learn to Play Drums with
Metallica
VOLUME 2

By Dan Gross

Recording Credits:
Jay Frederick, Drums
Karl Kaminski, Bass

Cover photo by Mark Leialoha

Cherry Lane Music Company
Educational Director/Project Supervisor: Susan Poliniak
Director of Publications: Mark Phillips
Manager of Publications: Gabrielle Fastman

ISBN-13: 978-1-57560-867-9
ISBN-10: 1-57560-867-7

Visit our website at www.cherrylane.com

CONTENTS

INTRODUCTION

Welcome to *Learn to Play Drums with Metallica: Volume 2.* Picking up where the first book left off, we'll be diving headlong into the essence of Master Ulrich's drumming wizardry. You may at times be astounded and confounded, but you'll come around as you joyfully pound those drums into submission.

Through examples from dozens of Metallica songs, the first book in this series introduced you to the building blocks of drumset notation, rhythm notation, counting, time feels, time signatures, and basic drumming rudiments. This volume takes it from there, guiding you step-by-step through intermediate and advanced patterns and concepts.

With a thorough analysis of the key technical and stylistic components of Lars' playing, you can begin to absorb not only his drumbeats but his approach to music as well. And you will come to understand and appreciate even more the significance of his contribution to the depth, strength, and sound that are Metallica.

ABOUT THE AUTHOR

Dan Gross

Dan Gross has been a professional drummer, percussionist, and educator for over 20 years. With extensive touring, performing, and recording work throughout the United States, Canada, Europe, and Asia, in a wide range of musical venues and styles from clubs to concert halls to the Broadway pit, Dan is fortunate to be able to draw from all of these experiences in his teaching and writing endeavors. He lives and works in—and out of—the New York City area.

ACKNOWLEDGMENTS

For their patience, guidance, and unfailing assistance during the writing of this book, Dan would like to acknowledge Susan Poliniak, the Educational Director at Cherry Lane Music and Jean-Pierre Perreaux for his on-call expert technical support. For everything else under the sun, Dan would like to thank his best friend and ceaselessly understanding wife, Rose.

CHAPTER 1

Battery—Gear Selection, Mechanics, Timekeeping, and Practice Approach

Gear Selection

Battery. Aside from being the title of a great Metallica track on *Master of Puppets*, the word refers, in symphonic terms, to the part of the percussion section that includes the concert bass drum, snare drum, tenor drum, and suspended and crash cymbals. Treated as separate entities in the orchestra, these dynamic voices were combined into a single instrument many years ago as a new American musical art form, jazz, grew from its infancy. The modern drumset has evolved in many ways over the years, and thanks to advances in manufacturing technology, the range of gear choices today is boundless. There are certain factors, however, that should help to steer you in making purchase decisions.

First, there is *price*. We don't all have unlimited budgets with which to satisfy our drum equipment cravings. Fortunately, there is gear available for all wallets. From entry level (student) to professional models and everything in between, there is a kit out there to suit every drummer's financial situation. Because the construction and sound quality of your gear will serve to inspire you to spend more time in the practice room, it is important to do your research and to ask questions of professionals, shop owners and employees, and fellow drum enthusiasts and students. Ultimately, you should buy the highest quality instruments that you can comfortably afford—even if that means saving up and buying your dream kit a few pieces at a time.

Second, consider the space in which you will be practicing. The available room will obviously have some bearing on your decisions, as will sound level restrictions. Though acoustic drums ("the real deal") are certainly preferred, there are good electronic drums on the market that can allow you, with a good set of isolation headphones, to fairly closely simulate the feel and sound of real drums while keeping the decibel level to a virtual hush.

And then there is the issue of musical style(s). The type of music you will be playing, too, plays a big role in your gear choices, particularly in terms of the drum sizes, drumhead choices, and cymbal selections. Though there are no hard and fast rules about these things, there are certain accepted norms to consider. Again, it's your music, your equipment, and your budget, so you make the call. Here are a few suggestions specific to playing metal and related styles.

Bass Drums

The big boys—24" in diameter is often preferred for this type of music, but 22" is an excellent all-around size. If you have the space for them and can afford two bass drums, preferably of the same size, then go for it. That's the ideal. If there is only one bass drum in your near future, that's okay. Read on to find out about double pedal options for a single bass drum.

Snare Drums

Something on the deeper side is preferable for metal—6.5", 7", or 8" in depth. Metal shells are often desired for metal music (go figure!) due to their cut-through crack, and Lars has a signature drum on the market.

Mounted (Rack) Toms

Over the years, Lars has used setups with one, two, three, or four toms over his bass drums. If you're using only one, 12" is a good all-purpose size. The standard combination for two toms is 12" and 13" in diameter. For three rack toms, it's 12", 13", and 14". For four toms, you could add a 10" on the top end or a 15" on the low end.

Floor Toms

A good way to go is with 16" and/or 18". If choosing only one floor tom, you might go with the "bigger is better" approach common to the style.

Cymbals

For the purposes of this book, you need a pair of hi-hat cymbals (14" standard), a ride cymbal (22" is standard for metal, though 20" and 24" are great options), and at least one crash cymbal. Particularly with the crash, you want something meaty and durable enough to stand up to metal. There are seemingly infinite choices for crash cymbals, but an 18" or 19" on the thicker side should serve you well.

Hardware

Decisions on hardware (stands, throne, pedals) are more crucial than you might think. A comfortable back-supporting seat or throne, and medium-weight cymbal stands (if you plan on moving your kit back and forth to rehearsals, shows, etc.) will spare you from multiple visits to the chiropractor and physical therapist. Spend extra time (and money, if necessary) on finding a smooth, quick, dependable bass drum pedal. Especially for working with the music of Metallica, a great pedal is an absolute necessity. Will you be playing one or two bass drums? If two, you will, of course, need two separate, single pedals; if one, there are a number of excellent double pedals (with two beaters designed to be played on one drum) on the market.

Mechanics

Always bear in mind that the drumset is a very personal and physical instrument. The type, quality, and arrangement of your drums, cymbals, and hardware each have a great effect on the way you play, the way you feel, and the way you sound. Extremely important, too, is your technique—the mechanics of the way you actually sit at and strike the instrument. The first *Learn to Play Drums with Metallica* book goes into good detail here with a number of solid tips. Suffice it to say that no matter which grip you choose for holding the sticks—traditional, matched, French, or some hybrid—tension is the enemy. Because metal drumming in particular is so physically demanding, it is very important that you remain relaxed and breathing comfortably at all times. There should always be an easy flow of energy from your shoulders and upper arms to your forearms, wrists, and fingers. The same flow should occur from your hips, thighs, and quadraceps to your knees, lower legs, and feet. To those ends, sit at a height at which you can maintain good posture (without slouching over, reaching too far, or turning your torso too much) while being able to play any part of your kit effortlessly. Note that a good private teacher is worth his or her weight in gold when it comes to mechanics such as these.

Timekeeping

A topic closely linked to mechanics is *timekeeping*. Although every instrumentalist and vocalist is ultimately responsible for developing his or her own sense of beat, pulse, and meter, the task of keeping the ensemble together at the proper speed usually falls to the drummer. It's just the nature of the beast. Solid, steady time should be a constant priority for the serious drummer.

As mentioned previously in regard to drumming mechanics, remaining physically relaxed is key. The more fluid your motions, the greater your ability to keep a steady time flow and avoid speeding up or slowing down. The most significant factor, though, is simply *focus*. Make solid timekeeping a priority in all of your practice sessions, jam sessions, band rehearsals, and performances.

To develop that focus, there is one more piece of gear that you must purchase: a metronome. This fancy little time-keeping device will be your challenger and supporter, your tormenter and your best friend. A metronome will guide you, provide you with goals for each day's practice, and always keep you honest in terms of playing at a consistent tempo. In order for it to do its job, though, a metronome must be on, audible, and followed. At least 75 percent of your practice time should be spent with the metronome, so keep it handy. Since you will likely drown it out with your drumming, buy a set of isolation headphones (and any necesary adapters for a metronome's tiny headphone jack) so that you will always be able to hear that tell-tale click while protecting your hearing from the damaging effects of decibel overexposure.

Remember, your bandmates will look to you as the Official Keeper of Time. Don't let them down. Develop your own internal clock by using, hearing, and following the metronome during all of your practice sessions.

Practice Approach for This Book . . . and Everything Else!

The best way to master the examples and exercises presented in this book is simply to imagine "infinite repeat signs" at either end of each. With your metronome set at a slow speed (perhaps half of the indicated tempo), loop the example repeatedly while taking care to count and play all of the rhythms as precisely as possible. At some point—and it might be five minutes or 50 depending on the difficulty of the music—muscle memory will begin to take over. This is the point at which your performance becomes smooth and fluid because your hands and feet have so completely learned what to do that you can begin to relax and just play intuitively. You no longer have to concentrate so hard about keeping the coordination, timing, and balance together.

Once you have achieved this state of practice bliss, increase the metronome speed slightly. A bump of four to eight b.p.m. (beats per minute) should be sufficient. Count, play, and repeat the example at this new tempo until it, too, becomes easy for you. Keep pushing the tempo little by little in this fashion until you hit a *wall*—a speed that is just too fast for you to play cleanly. Stop and work on something else for a while. When you come back to this one later on in the day or the next day, chances are that your mind/limb connection will have absorbed the pattern and you will be able to push the envelope and increase your top speed a bit. Go for it. Just try to keep everything as relaxed and solid as possible. When you have command of the example at the designated tempo, try playing along with the accompanying CD. Perhaps you might want to cue up the Metallica recording and play the longer examples along with Lars and the band!

A word to the wise: Whenever beginning work on a new beat, fill, technique, or musical passage, be sure to take a minute or two with the metronome to count out the rhythms carefully. This first step is the most important. If you learn something incorrectly from the beginning and practice it that way, you'll simply reinforce the mistake. To paraphrase the title of a Metallica song, the "The (Muscle) Memory Remains"—and you will have to do double duty unlearning the mistake and then learning the correction. Those extra few minutes spent at the start are well worth it.

If you find an example particularly challenging to put together at first, break it down into smaller sections. Try one measure at a time—or even one beat at a time—and slowly piece it together. If it's not the amount of music but the complexity that poses the difficulty, scale the example down to its simplest form and build from there. For instance, if there are too many notes to digest all at once, leave a few out until you can easily play the "skeleton" of the music. Once you are comfortable with that, add the rest of the notes back in, one at a time if necessary, before concerning yourself with speed. Always remember—*slow it down and break it down*. The care and discipline you use when learning something new will pay big dividends in results down the line.

CHAPTER 2

Jump in the Fire—A Review of Notation and Other Basics

Rhythmic Notation

Let's get started with a brief review of some reading essentials that you will need for this book. In order to get the most out of *Learn to Play Drums with Metallica: Volume 2* and to make the most efficient use of your practice time, it is important to have a good working knowledge and understanding of music notation. If you have never read music before or are simply a bit rusty, take some time to bring these skills up to par. The stronger your reading *chops* (skills) are, the more you can focus your practice time on actually playing the written examples in this book. The first book in this series provides excellent practical studies in rhythmic notation, and a few lessons with a private instructor can help tremendously in getting your reading together.

Learning how to *count* rhythms properly is essential to quickly learning how to *play* them properly. Assuming that you already know what the different notes and rests look like, here is a short counting tutorial to get you started.

First, take a look at the following chart. One whole note is the same duration as two half notes, one half note is the same duration as two quarter notes, one quarter note equals two eighth notes, one eighth note equals two 16th notes, and one 16th note equals two 32nd notes. The same scenario holds for the equivalent rests.

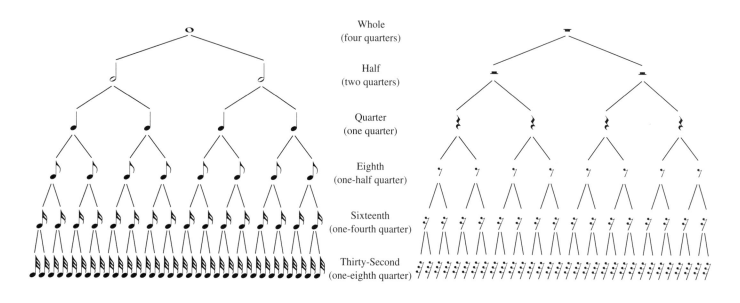

For now, we will use a time signature of 4/4, or *common time*. Although Metallica's music often explores other time signatures, 4/4 is still the default setting, if you will. In a time signature, the top number (here, "4") indicates the number of beats per measure; so we know that we should count up to four in each measure. The bottom number (here, "4" again) indicates the type of note whose *value* (length) is equal to one of those beats. In 4/4 time, each quarter note is one beat long—or, as we say, the quarter note "gets one beat." In 4/4 time, the different note types from the chart are counted as follows.

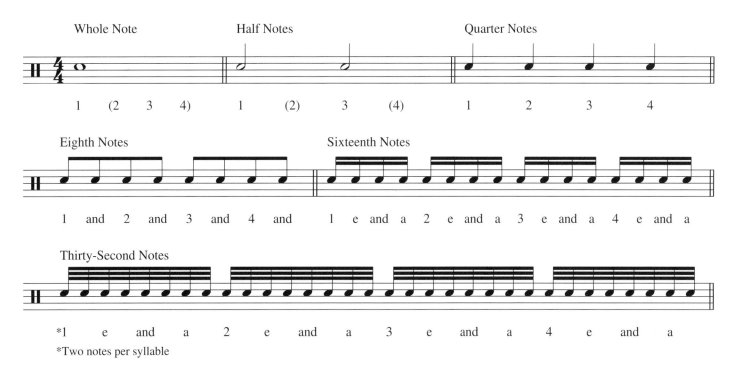

Thus far, everything has been based on multiples of two. However, notes and rests can appear in groups of three called *triplets*. Essentially, when you see a triplet (notated by a small numeral "3" above a group of three notes, rests, or a combination thereof), this indicates that the three notes should be played so that they fit into the same space (i.e., time period) in which two notes would normally be played.

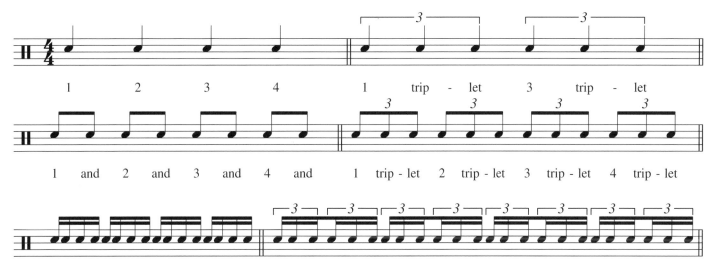

Here's one more for the road—a *dot* placed after a note increases the duration of that note by half. For example, a plain old half note gets two beats (is two beats in length). Half of two is one, and two plus one equals three; therefore, a dotted half note gets three beats. Various common dotted note configurations are counted like this.

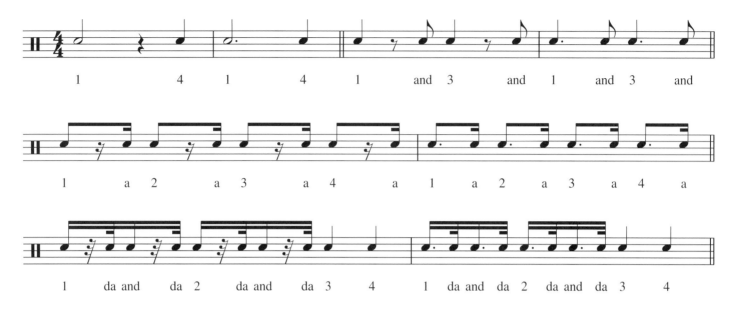

Drumset Notation Key

The various parts of the drumset are notated throughout this volume as shown on the notation key below. Though Lars changed his setup occasionally, this key covers all of the examples and exercises in the book.

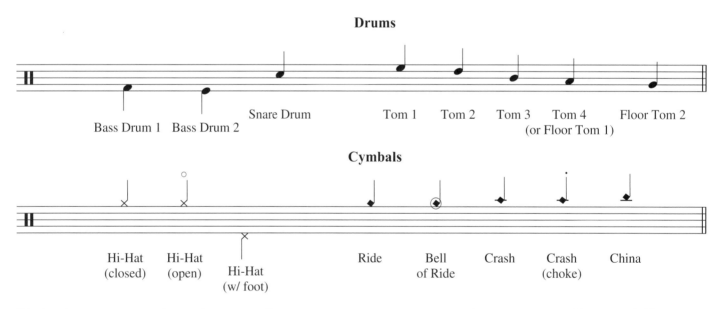

Obviously, you may need to make some adjustments or compromises to match your own tom/floor tom/effects cymbals (splash/China) setup. Here's the minimal setup that you need to work your way through this book. Everything else is gravy!

- Two bass drums (or one bass drum with a double pedal)
- One snare drum
- One mounted or rack tom (preferably two or more)
- One floor tom
- One pair of hi-hat cymbals
- One ride cymbal
- One crash cymbal
- One drum throne

Tempo Markings

Tempo markings are supplied with each example and indicate the speed of the original Metallica recording. To practice, start much more slowly than this tempo (no more than half of the indicated speed) and gradually work your way up to and, if humanly possible, beyond the recording tempos.

Reading Examples

To make the best use of your time, make sure that you have a thorough grasp of note values and counting before continuing on with the main body of this book. There is some challenging technical material ahead, and the better your reading is now, the more you can focus on coordination, time, and feel. To get an idea of where you're at with this, set the metronome at a slow speed and try reading/counting/playing through the next few examples. If you find that you are having considerable difficulty figuring them out, that's alright—you may want to check out the first *Learn to Play Drums with Metallica* book before continuing here. If you have little or no trouble with them, then please proceed into the mighty world of Lars Ulrich's impressive drumming style and technique!

For the purpose of this reading exercise, count and play the following example with even eighth notes—"1–and–2–and–3–and–4–and." On the actual Metallica recording, however, the eighth notes are played with a *triplet feel* (also called a *swing feel*). Later in this chapter, you will see how the triplet feel completely alters the way this example sounds.

"2 x 4" Chorus from *Load*

Words and Music by James Hetfield, Lars Ulrich and Kirk Hammett
Copyright © 1996 Creeping Death Music (ASCAP)
International Copyright Secured   All Rights Reserved

Try this on for size—a short excerpt in (ready?) 5/4.

"Blackened" Interlude from . . . *And Justice for All*

TRACK 02

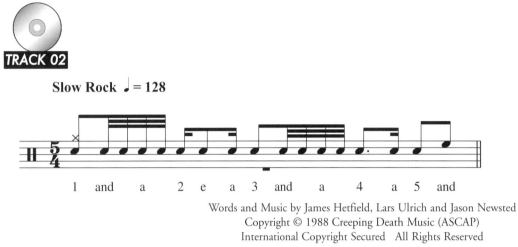

As long as the bottom number of the time signature is 4, then all of the same note values and counting rules from 4/4 apply. The only difference is the number of beats in each measure.

Compound meters, or time signatures based on subdivisions of three instead of two, are more common on Metallica's later albums. For instance, in a meter such as 12/8, a dotted quarter note is felt as the main pulse or beat instead of a quarter note. Each dotted quarter pulse is subdivided into a group of three eighth notes. Count along with the metronome as you read the following examples. Notice how compound meters have a sway to them due to the subdivision of three. At slow tempi, 12/8 can be treated as 12 counts of eighth notes as the time signature implies; however, generally in this style of music, 12/8 time is counted and felt as four beats with three eighth notes in each. Likewise, a two-count is commonly used for 6/8 time.

"Don't Tread on Me" Intro from *Metallica*

TRACK 03

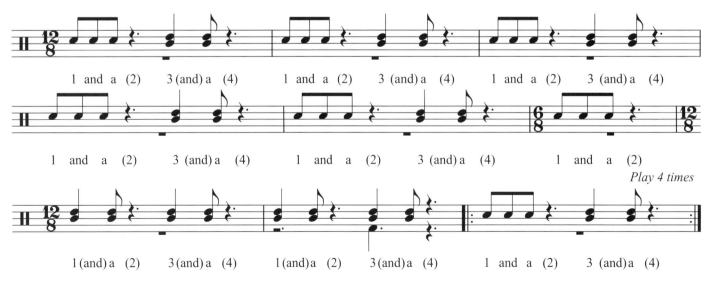

1 and a (2) 3 (and) a (4) a 1 and a 2 and a 3 and a 4 and a

You may even encounter time signatures with a top number of 7, 9, or 11. Take a look at the following example. The first four measures are in 4/4, but the next measure is in 7/8 (the last one is in good ol' 2/4). Don't worry—7/8 is just like a 4/4 bar without the final eighth note. If you're having problems getting the feel of that measure, make sure to count out the eighth notes.

"Disposable Heroes" Chorus from *Master of Puppets*

1 and trip-let 2 and 3 and 4 and (1) and 2 3 and 4 and 1 and 2 3 and 4 and

1 and 2 3 and 4 1 2 trip-let 3 4 5 6 7 1 (and 2 and)

Words and Music by James Hetfield, Lars Ulrich and Kirk Hammett
Copyright © 1986 Creeping Death Music (ASCAP)
International Copyright Secured All Rights Reserved

Don't be discouraged if all of this counting seems like one, big, annoying, intellectual exercise. It is, but by practicing counting and feeling these complicated rhythms and odd time signatures, you can gain a comfort level with the more difficult side of Metallica's work. This effort can open up a whole new world for you as a player, so stick with it.

Time Feels

But let's get back to 4/4, if you don't mind. Throughout this book, you'll encounter time feels such as *straight time*, *half-time feel, double-time feel,* and *triplet feel.* These terms simply describe the way the drum parts sound and the rate of motion they imply. You can read and count them just as they are written on the page. But subtle differences from one drum beat, or groove, to another—in the placement of the snare drum notes, for example—can create wonderful variety in the way the drum patterns *feel* to the listener.

When the groove feels like the 4/4 rock pattern to which our ears are most accustomed (essentially with beats 1 and 3 played on the bass drum and beats 2 and 4 played on the snare drum), we refer to this as *straight time.* When the snare is played only on beat 3 (instead of on beats 2 and 4), we refer to this as a *half-time feel* because this gives the listener the impression that the music is now at half speed. When, however, the snare is played on all of the *upbeats* (all of the "ands"), we call this a *double-time feel* because, although the pulses and our counting are still going by at the same speed, the snare drum notes make us feel as though the music is now twice as fast.

Lars and the band often switch feels in the middle of a song, and sometimes from one measure to the next. This example goes from straight time with a big fill leading into a half-time section that also ends with a fill.

"The Thorn Within" Chorus/Guitar Solo from *Load*

On occasion, music may be written with plain old eighth notes with an indication above the music that reads *triplet feel.* This should be played with that loping, subdivision-of-three feel akin to 12/8.

Let's take another look at that earlier example from the song, "2 x 4." This time, count and play it with the proper triplet feel in which each pair of written eighth notes should be played as though they were the outer two (first and third) notes of an eighth note triplet.

"2 x 4" Second Chorus from *Load*

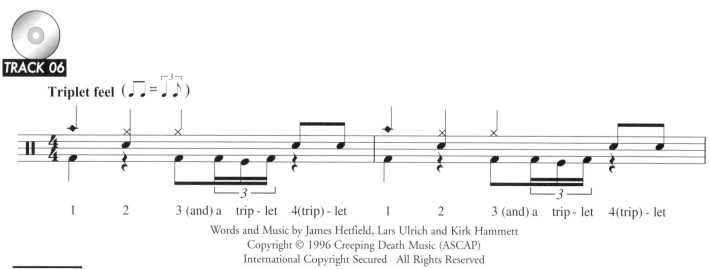

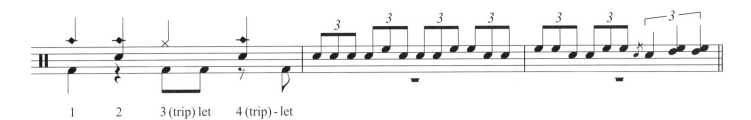

Listen to this track on the CD, and compare it to the earlier version played with an even (i.e., normal) eighth note feel. It's a subtle timing shift in the eighth notes, but it gives an entirely different feeling to the groove.

Rudiments

Rudiments are the ABCs of drumming—the essential elements that make up much of what we do with the sticks. They run the gamut from basic *single-stroke rolls* (RLRLRLRL or LRLRLRLR, etc.) and *double-stroke rolls* (RRLLR-RLL or LLRRLLRR, etc.) to *paradiddles* (RLRR or LRLL), *flams, ruffs,* and many other more complicated sticking combinations. Lars uses only a few of the standard rudiments in his playing—and these only on occasion. Thus, this book is not the proper forum for an in-depth examination of them. Ask around for a good rudimental text—or better yet, find a teacher with a solid rudimental background. The more you know, the more armed and dangerous you are behind the kit. For our purposes here, though, a brief review of flams and ruffs will suffice.

A *flam* is a simple two-stroke rudiment in which the two notes are played almost, but not quite, simultaneously. In the classic rudimental style, the first (smaller) note is called a *grace note* and is played more softly (with a shorter stroke) than the second (larger) *principal note.* Rock 'n' roll flams, though, are generally played with both notes at roughly the same stroke height and volume. Experiment with different height/volume relationships between the two notes until you find the balance that suits your taste best. And remember to practice flams with either hand playing the lead or grace note.

"Holier Than Thou" Intro from *Metallica*

TRACK 07

Moderately fast Rock ♩ = 166

On a few songs, Lars slips in a *ruff* or two. Ruffs are similar to flams, but they contain two grace notes that precede a principal note. The two grace notes should be played with the same hand as one short, downward wrist stroke plus a bounce or rebound, rather than as two separate wrist strokes. The stronger principal note is played with the other hand (LLR or RRL).

"Poor Twisted Me" Verse from *Load*

Dynamic and Form Markings

Dynamic markings express the volume, or loudness, at which to play. Though Metallica's music generally requires the use of the upper range of dynamics, try practicing everything in this book at varying degrees of volume. You will find that mixing in some softer playing (especially when working on fast, challenging passages) can greatly improve your touch, control, and flow around the drumkit.

Here are some common dynamic markings with their full Italian meanings and English translations.

pp	pianissimo	very soft
p	piano	soft
mp	mezzo piano	medium soft
mf	mezzo forte	medium loud
f	forte	loud
ff	fortissimo	very loud

For us drummers, it is an absolute necessity that we understand song form—the manner in which various sections of music are ordered and joined to create a song structure. Intro, verse, pre-chorus, bridge, solo, interlude, coda and outro are all common *form markings* with which we should be familiar. Understanding song form helps us to know when to fill, set up new sections of music, and guide the rest of the band. And should you decide to advance your Lars Ulrich/Metallica studies beyond *Learn to Play Drums with Metallica: Volume 2*, Cherry Lane's note-for-note drum transcription books contain complete drum parts with thorough form indications.

CHAPTER 3

Ride the Lightning—Cymbal and Floor Tom Ride Patterns

Standard Cymbal Ride Patterns

Typically in most rock beats, the lead hand (e.g., the right hand for a right-handed drummer) will *ride* or play a repetitive rhythm to provide a backdrop for the bass drum/snare drum pattern. This ride rhythm is most often a simple, steady stream of quarter or eighth notes played on open (often notated as "o") or closed ("+") hi-hats or on the ride cymbal.

For example, in the song "No Remorse" from Metallica's first album, Lars plays a quarter note pattern on the hi-hat in the verse and a quarter note pattern on the ride cymbal in the chorus.

"No Remorse" Verse from *Kill 'Em All*

TRACK 09

Fast Rock ♩ = 188

Words and Music by James Hetfield and Lars Ulrich
Copyright © 1983 Creeping Death Music (ASCAP)
International Copyright Secured   All Rights Reserved

"No Remorse" Chorus from *Kill 'Em All*

TRACK 10

Fast Rock ♩ = 188

Words and Music by James Hetfield and Lars Ulrich
Copyright © 1983 Creeping Death Music (ASCAP)
International Copyright Secured   All Rights Reserved

In "Seek and Destroy" from the same album, Lars uses an eighth note ride pattern for the first two vocal sections of the song—on the hi-hat for the verse and on the ride cymbal for the pre-chorus. Although the eighth note patterns use twice the number of notes per measure (eight) as the quarter note paterns in "No Remorse" (four), the tempo on "Seek and Destroy" is considerably slower (140 b.p.m.) than that of "No Remorse" (quarter note = 188). Though still quite fast, the patterns are completely playable with a little practice.

The *repeat signs* (bold line/thin line/two dots and two dots/thin line/bold line) that bracket measures 9–12 of this example indicate a repeat of the music that lies between those signs. Ordinarily, you would simply play bars 9 through 12 a second time. In this case, however, there are *first and second endings* at the 12th and 13th measures. So, the road map for the example is as follows.

1. Play measures 1–8.

2. Continuing on (notice the repeat sign), play measures 9–11 and then measure 12 (the first ending) before taking the repeat back to measure 9.

3. For a second time, play measures 9–11.

4. Now, skip over (do not play) the first ending (measure 12) and jump to the second ending (measure 13) before continuing on with the last measure.

Follow along as you listen to the recorded track a few times and this should all become very clear.

"Seek & Destroy" Verse/Pre-Chorus from *Kill 'Em All*

Though more common at slower *tempi* (Italian, plural form of *tempo*), 16th notes can also be used for ride patterns, as in the following fast-handed example. By beginning the 16ths with the right hand on beat 2 of the first measure and alternating the sticking (RLRL, etc.), Lars plays the snare drum backbeats (strong hits on beats 2 and 4) with his right hand and never has to cross one hand over or under the other.

"Jump in the Fire" Chorus from *Kill 'Em All*

Words and Music by James Hetfield, Lars Ulrich and Dave Mustaine
Copyright © 1983 Creeping Death Music (ASCAP)
International Copyright Secured   All Rights Reserved

Now, although the 16th notes make this a very "busy" beat, the chorus of this particular song has very few lyrics, so Lars' note-filled pattern never gets in the way of James Hetfield's vocals. It just adds a wonderful frenetic energy to the section.

So far, as you may have noticed, you've seen only ride patterns from *Kill 'Em All*. While Lars continued to make extensive use of these standard cymbal patterns on all of the later recordings, his drumming vocabulary expanded tremendously beginning with the band's sophomore effort, *Ride the Lightning*. And so will yours as you work your way through this book! Like Lars, as you take more command of the instrument, you can gain the dexterity, strength, and independence between the limbs that will allow you to mix things up a bit on the fly.

For example, in the first verse of "Ronnie" from *Load*, Lars plays a relatively simple groove with a 16th note hi-hat ride pattern broken up occasionally by a few eighth notes.

"Ronnie" Verse from *Load*

Moderately slow Rock ♩ = 92

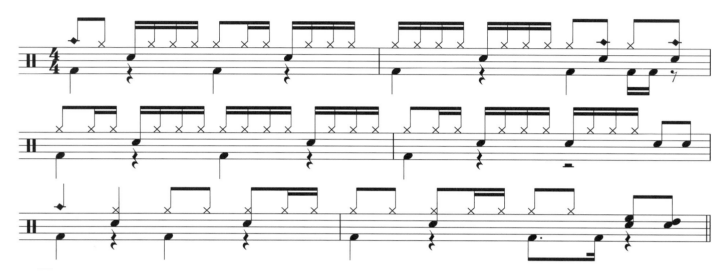

Conversely, he plays an eighth note pattern with a few 16ths thrown in on "Slither."

"Slither" Verse from *ReLoad*

TRACK 14

♩ = 112

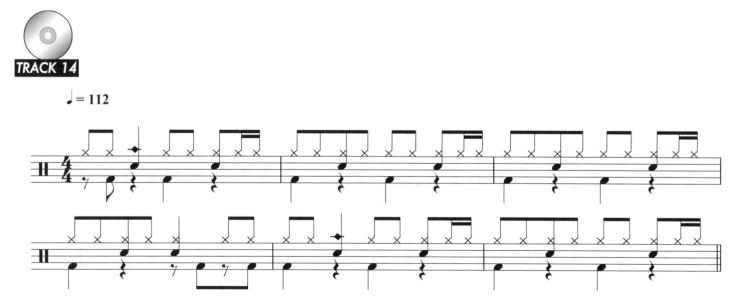

As you can hear on the accompanying CD and on the original recording, it's a minor change that adds a lot to the feel of the verse.

You will no doubt come across many other "broken" cymbal ride patterns like these in later chapters and future studies. The more comfortable you become with each of the standard cymbal ride patterns, the more you can begin to experiment with moving freely from one to another. For now, though, let's move on to another well-documented aspect of rock drumming—playing the ride pattern on the floor tom.

Floor Tom Ride Patterns

Like many great hard rock and metal drummers, Lars makes brilliant, creative use of riding on the floor tom for a heavier, darker, more primeval feel. There are a few fine examples of this on Metallica's first four albums, but Lars really begins to tap the vast potential of floor tom ride patterns from *Metallica* on.

One of the most straightforward yet amazingly effective examples of this is in the intro to "Enter Sandman." After eight bars of light cymbal time, Lars kicks the song into gear. Played in straight 4/4 time, he simply lays down quarter notes on the bass drum, backbeats (2 and 4) on tom 4 instead of on the snare drum, and punctuates the guitar chord anticipations at the end of each four-measure phrase with the snare and crash cymbal. The section ends with an eighth note build into the verse groove. It's basic, but, man, does it rock!

"Enter Sandman" Intro from *Metallica*

Words and Music by James Hetfield, Lars Ulrich and Kirk Hammett
Copyright © 1991 Creeping Death Music (ASCAP)
International Copyright Secured   All Rights Reserved

Here's a nifty little groove in which the right hand moves back and forth from the floor tom to the snare and the left hand moves from the snare to tom 2. Lars uses this one on "Cure" at the end of each pre-chorus and again in the interlude before the final chorus.

"Cure" Pre-Chorus from *Load*

Finally, as we're kicking the intensity up a notch, we'll finish this chapter with two floor tom grooves from the early days when Master Ulrich was much more inclined to abuse *two* bass drum heads at a time instead of just one. At the end of the bridge in "Trapped Under Ice," just before the third guitar solo (What?! Two solos in one song ain't enough?), Lars plays a quarter note floor tom ride pattern over his trademark double bass 16ths at a moderately fast clip (moderately fast for early Metallica, that is).

"Trapped Under Ice" Bridge from *Ride the Lightning*

And now for a killer! About halfway into the intro to "Harvester of Sorrow," Lars starts playing the following beat. For the first phrase of six measures, he rides not on the floor tom but on tom 3. He moves the right hand to the floor tom for the next six-measure phrase, which is what you see below. The tempo is not fast, and all of that black ink makes it look a lot nastier than it is, but what is so impressive here is Lars' complete control of his bass drums. The ease with which he sets up the basic groove and then drops in double bass 16th note triplets or 32nd notes or 32nd note triplets wherever and whenever he pleases is just amazing! If you look closely, you'll see that only once does Lars play exactly the same measure twice in a row.

"Harvester of Sorrow" Intro from . . . *And Justice for All*

Slow Rock ♩ = 84

A bit of a challenge, huh? No worries, mate. If you're finding this one difficult to put together, remember—*slow it down and break it down.* I would suggest first working on the feet alone. Go slowly, and count carefully along with the metronome. If you can't count it or feel it/hear it in your head, you'll have a tougher time learning to play it. And don't be too concerned if your double bass drum technique isn't quite together yet. You will be getting plenty of practice later in this book. When you've got the feet down, add just the right-hand floor tom part. Once you're totally solid on that, then and only then should you try to fill in the left hand. You'll get it. This one just might take some patience and doggedness.

You can find a number of other examples of floor tom ride patterns in Metallica's music. Listen to other bands and drummers, too, and spend some of your practice time just playing and inventing your own versions of this time-honored staple of rock drumming.

Good luck, and I'll see you in the next chapter.

CHAPTER 4

Wherever the Snare May Roam—Half-Time Feels, Straight-Time Feels, and Shadowed Backbeats

Similar to the way the left-foot hi-hat can function in jazz, it is the placement of the snare drum backbeats in rock drumming that generally determines the overall feel of the groove. As you know, when playing a straight time 4/4 beat, the snare is usually played on beats 2 and 4. For a half-time feel, a single snare hit is played on beat 3. And playing consistent snare notes on all four upbeats—the "ands"—creates a double time feel. These three snare patterns are far and away the most commonly heard in Metallica's music.

However, there will be occasions in which you, as the drummer, will want to try something a bit different—something out of the ordinary. And, as you are about to see, you can achieve this by simply displacing, or moving, some or all of the snare backbeats.

In the intro to "No Remorse," Lars starts to lay down a standard half-time feel, but every other bar (the second, fourth, and sixth measures) has a snare hit on beat 4 instead of beat 3. Notice, too, that in the fifth measure, Lars momentarily switches to a straight-time feel with the snare played on 2 and 4. It's an interesting mix of feels in one section of music, and it's all due to the variety of snare placements.

"No Remorse" Intro from *Kill 'Em All*

Words and Music by James Hetfield and Lars Ulrich
Copyright © 1983 Creeping Death Music (ASCAP)
International Copyright Secured   All Rights Reserved

Here's a great little half-time feel variation. It's a cool two-bar phrase in which the backbeat in the second bar is "anticipated." In other words, the snare note in the second measure is moved up, or played a half a beat *ahead* of where it would normally be (on the "and" of beat 2 instead of beat 3).

"King Nothing" Pre-Chorus from *Load*

Moderately ♩ = 120
Half-time feel

Words and Music by James Hetfield, Lars Ulrich and Kirk Hammett
Copyright © 1996 Creeping Death Music (ASCAP)
International Copyright Secured   All Rights Reserved

While we're looking at "King Nothing," Lars plays a *shadowed,* or doubled, backbeat groove in the latter half of the bridge section of the song. Though not actually *moving* the backbeat, but rather *adding* extra snare notes on the "e" of 2 and the "e" of 4, this does add a new wrinkle to the standard straight-time feel.

"King Nothing" Bridge from *Load*

Moderately ♩ = 120

Play 4 times

Words and Music by James Hetfield, Lars Ulrich and Kirk Hammett
Copyright © 1996 Creeping Death Music (ASCAP)
International Copyright Secured   All Rights Reserved

These examples should give you a few ideas on how to change up your grooves through simple backbeat displacement. Another way to approach it is to start with one of your favorite beats—one that you play often and with which you feel completely comfortable. Now, try to move one of the snare notes ahead or back, or even remove it altogether. Presto! You've just created a new groove variation. Now, try a different change in the snare pattern. Exhaust all of the possibilities. Some will feel and sound great and be musically useful. Others simply will have served as good exercises. Repeat the process with other beats that you tend to play, and you will have greatly expanded your groove vocabulary!

CHAPTER 5

Slither—Shuffle Grooves

Most contemporary rock and pop music is in either a *duple feel* (based on groups of two) or a *triple feel* (based on groups of three). For example, your basic 4/4 rock beat with even eighth notes on the hi-hat is in duple meter, with two eighth notes per beat (see Example A below). But some grooves are based on a rhythm of three notes per beat. These can be writen in 4/4 time as one eighth note triplet per beat (B) or in 12/8 time with three eighth notes per beat (C).

TRACK 22

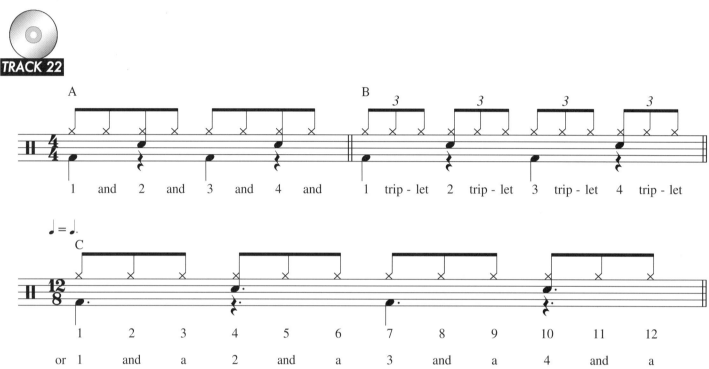

Because of the three-note groupings, the grooves in B and C have a loping, swinging character to them. Now, playing all three notes of a triplet in every beat is alright as long as the tempo is a slow or moderate one. But even if you happen to have very fast hands, this riding pattern on the cymbal can make the overall drumbeat seem cluttered at higher speeds. So try omitting the second, or middle, note of each triplet. In other words, play only the first and third—"outer"—notes of each group of three as in D below.

TRACK 23

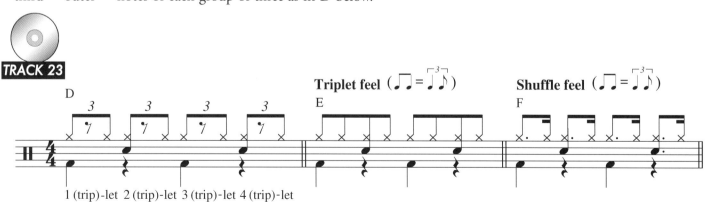

To achieve the proper feel for the beat in Example D, imagine how your gait would sound (just bear with me now) if you had an injured leg. You would be "shuffling" down the street. So these grooves are called *shuffles* because of the feel created by the triplets, especially when the middle notes are omitted. Example E above is simply a common notational shorthand for a desired shuffle groove. Although written with straight eighth notes rather than triplets in the cymbal part, there is an indication that these eighths are to be played with a triplet feel, or *swung*, as if they were the outer notes of an eighth note triplet.

Occasionally, you might run into something like Example F in which the cymbal part is written with dotted eighth note/16th note combinations. Because the instruction "shuffle feel" is written here, this beat should be played more loosely than the strict "**1**–e–and–**a**–**2**–e–and–**a**–**3**–e–and–**a**–**4**–e–and–**a**" rhythm shown. In effect, Examples D, E, and F are to be played and should sound exactly the same. As you gain more experience as a drummer, you will find that changing the amount of swing used in a beat can create wonderful subtle variations in a shuffle feel. For now, though, just concentrate on getting a smooth, rolling triplet feel from the following examples from The Man Himself.

There are a number of ways to approach shuffles on the drums, and we'll start with the simplest of all—just let the guitarists do it! In the first *Learn to Play Drums with Metallica* book, Chapter 8 includes examples from the intro and chorus of "For Whom the Bell Tolls." But Lars breaks it down even further in the verse. He plays the simplest "skeleton" quarter note beat and lets the triplet figures in the bass and guitars create the shuffle feel. Only in the fills at the end of each four-measure phrase does Lars actually play any triplets.

"For Whom the Bell Tolls" Verse from *Ride the Lightning*

TRACK 24

Moderate Rock ♩ = 120

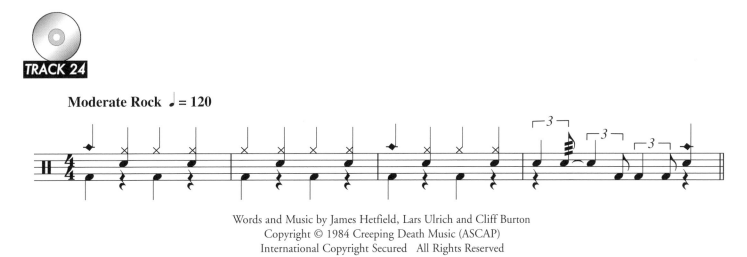

This is a very streamlined way to play a shuffle that leaves a lot of space in the music. Yes, it's "easy," but it takes considerable musical maturity, taste, and discipline to be so selective.

But let's say that you want to imply the shuffle feel more in the drumset part. Remember Examples B and E?

"2 x 4" Second Verse from *Load*

TRACK 25

Moderate Rock ♩ = 112

Triplet feel (♫ = ♩♪)

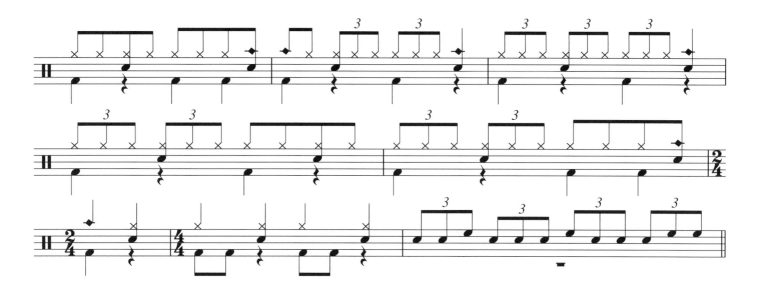

Or you can play quarter notes in the cymbal riding pattern and let the bass drum, or even the left hand snare/tom parts, play the shuffled eighth notes. This is exactly what Lars does from the final section of the chorus (bass drum shuffling) to the half-time feel guitar solo (mixed bass drum and snare/tom shuffling).

"2 x 4" Chorus/Guitar Solo from *Load*

TRACK 26

Half-time feel

How about playing the triplets in your feet on two bass drums? If you have only a single pedal now, then this will be a great exercise for speed and endurance as you play all of the notes with one foot. If you do have a double pedal, then go for it—and know that you're going to get a serious, leg-burning, double bass workout in the chapters ahead!

"The Four Horsemen" First Verse from *Kill 'Em All*

Fast Rock ♩ = 204

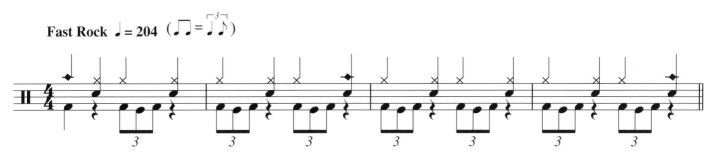

Words and Music by James Hetfield, Lars Ulrich and Dave Mustaine
Copyright © 1983 Creeping Death Music (ASCAP)
International Copyright Secured   All Rights Reserved

Here's a great example of making quick, smooth transitions from a duple to a triple feel and back. The verse of "Eye of the Beholder" is in a straight duple feel with steady double bass 16ths. Since we will be covering Lars' double bass drum playing in detail later on, if you can't tackle it at this point, just play a simpler single bass drum pattern in the first four measures for now. This example starts in the fifth bar of the second verse (with the lyric "Do you take what I take?"). Lars plays a two-beat triplet fill to make the move from the even duple feel to the triplet feel of the 12/8 section. He grooves on a shuffle for a bit before playing an even eighth/16th note fill ("and–4–and–1–e–and–2–e–and") to lead us back into a straight steady 4/4 beat.

"Eye of the Beholder" Second Verse from . . . *And Justice for All*

Words and Music by James Hetfield, Lars Ulrich and Kirk Hammett
Copyright © 1988 Creeping Death Music (ASCAP)
International Copyright Secured   All Rights Reserved

Nailing these transitions is a little tougher than you might think at first, so be patient and really work at it. Focus on making your shuffle grooves and fills as fluid and smooth as possible. Because that magical swaying feel of the shuffle can be elusive, spend as much time as possible listening to these tracks on the accompanying CD—and, of course, to the original Metallica recordings.

CHAPTER 6

Getting Off on the Right Foot—Single Bass Drum 16th Note Pairs and Triplets

One of the prime requisites for playing the music of Metallica is a lightning-fast bass drum foot. And Lars sure has that covered! This chapter focuses on single bass drum exercises and musical examples that can strengthen and quicken your foot and prepare you for the all-out double bass assault in later chapters. Once you have worked through all of the material in this chapter with your stronger lead foot (for most of us, the right foot), go back and try it with your non-dominant foot. Doing this can help to level the playing field for your double bass work.

On the band's first two albums, *Kill 'Em All* and *Ride the Lightning*, Lars actually played very little double bass, using it only when necessary for a long series of 16th notes. Otherwise, all of those amazing litle flurries of 16th note pairs and triplets were played with one foot! So do some ankle and calf stretches (I'm not kidding!) and let's dig in.

First, get loose and ready by sitting at the kit and playing pairs of bass drum strokes. Start slowly, stay relaxed, and take care that both strokes in each pair are dynamically as even as possible. Neither stroke should be significantly louder or "cleaner" sounding than the other. Slowly, decrease the space between the two notes in each pair. In other words, play the pairs faster, or closer together. Ideally, the two strokes should come one immediately after the other without losing the sound of two distinct notes. Now, try the same warm-up exercise with triplets by playing groups of three equally strong notes. Again, start slowly, and be sure that all three notes come out as clear, distinct, and strong as possible. Also, listen to the spacing (the aural "distance") between the strokes. Rhythmically, it should be exactly the same between the first and second notes as between the second and third. Work at playing each triplet more quickly, more tightly, and without losing volume or evenness. Your feet should feel tired by now. Take a short break by walking around for a minute. Do a little more stretching. Now, you're ready.

This first example of single bass drum 16th note pairs is fairly straight-ahead: 4/4 time with snare drum backbeats on 2 and 4. It is quite fast, though, at 184 b.p.m. It has some nice *anticipations* (measures 2, 3, and 7) in which the bass drum lands at the end of a measure instead of squarely on the downbeat of the next one (generally, this is done to match the harmonic rhythm of the chord changes in the guitars).

"Creeping Death" Guitar Solo from *Ride the Lightning*

Sixteenth note bass drum pairs can also work well with straight quarter notes on the snare drum. Try playing that excerpt from "Creeping Death" with snare drum notes on all four beats as follows.

Lars integrates these fast bass drum 16th pairs into half time feels on songs such as "Ride the Lightning" and "The Call of Ktulu."

"Ride the Lightning" Guitar Solo from *Ride the Lightning*

Moderate Rock ♩ = 150

Words and Music by James Hetfield, Lars Ulrich, Cliff Burton and Dave Mustaine
Copyright © 1984 Creeping Death Music (ASCAP)
International Copyright Secured   All Rights Reserved

Here's a groove you can find all over the place in Metallica's music.

"Phantom Lord" Intro from *Kill 'Em All*

Moderate Rock ♩ = 108

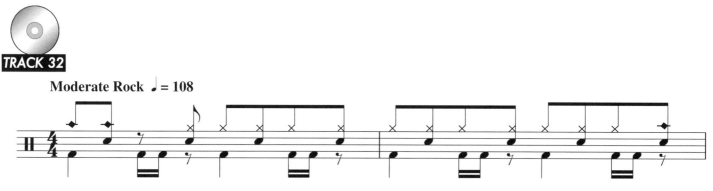

Words and Music by James Hetfield, Lars Ulrich and Dave Mustaine
Copyright © 1983 Creeping Death Music (ASCAP)
International Copyright Secured   All Rights Reserved

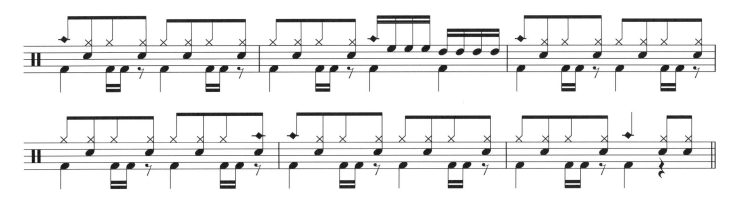

Before moving on, go back through the above examples using your other (weaker) foot to play the bass drum 16th pairs. You may struggle a bit, but this is good practice in preparation for the use of two bass drums later on in this book.

Okay . . . triplets, anyone?

In analyzing Lars' playing from the band's earliest releases, there is no question as to the most common single technical element—the bass drum triplet, three notes played in rapid succession on a single pedal. Lars uses this figure copiously—on almost every track of *Kill 'Em All*, in fact. And by applying his standard array of variations on top (in the hands), he creates plenty of interest to keep us mesmerized. So if you thought that the 16th pairs were challenging . . .

First, a quick reminder about counting/feeling 16th note triplets. Simply put, just as two 16th notes fit into the space of one eighth note, a 16th note triplet fits into that same space. In the example below, Example A should be counted "1–and–2–and–3–and–4–and" while B should be counted "1–and–a–2–and–3–and–a–4–and."

TRACK 33

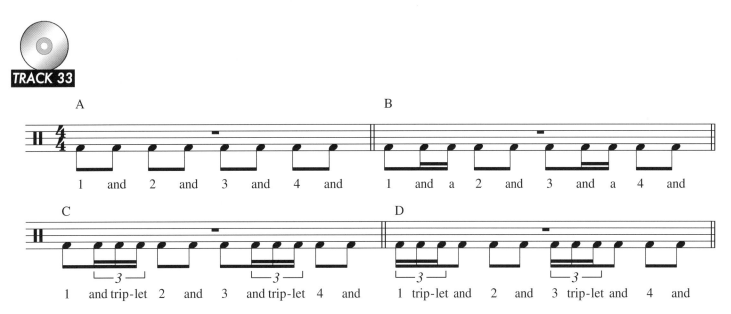

Example C is counted "1–and–trip-let–2–and–3–and–trip-let–4–and" while D is, in a sense, the reverse of Example C. The triplets in D fall on the downbeats instead of the upbeats and are counted "1–trip-let–and–2–and–3–trip-let–and–4–and."

To prepare your bass drum foot for the rigors of imitating Lars, let's start with a few exercises. Be precise in your counting and execution as you play through these. Gradually increase the metronome speed, and don't be afraid to sweat a little!

Now, it's time to put your counting and technique into context. Here's a basic straight-time example with single bass drum triplets.

"(Anesthesia)—Pulling Teeth" Riff from *Kill 'Em All*

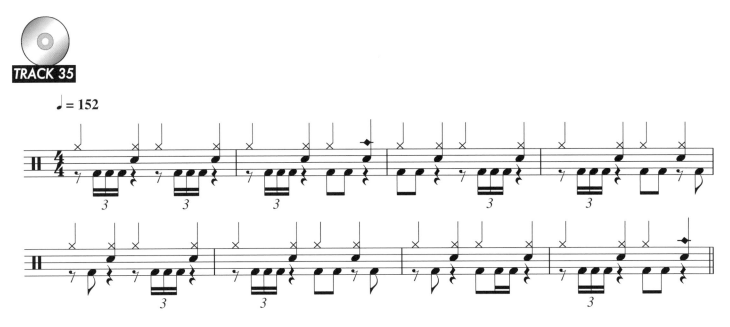

With Lars' famous quarter notes on the snare drum, we get the following.

"Jump in the Fire" Outro from *Kill 'Em All*

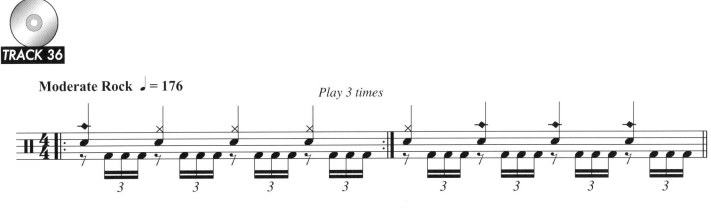

Occasionally, Lars uses bass drum triplets in a half-time feel. Don't let the 32nd note triplets throw you. The concept is similar to that of 16th note triplets. Instead of fitting three notes (a 16th note triplet) in the space of one eighth note, you fit a 32nd note triplet (still three notes) into the space of one 16th note (which equals two 32nd notes).

"The Four Horsemen" Bridge from *Kill 'Em All*

Puzzled? Fear not! The tempo here is much slower than in the previous examples, so the third beat of the first measure is simply counted "3–e–and–a–trip-let." Count 16ths along with the recorded example on the CD until you start to feel the 32nd note triplets; then, get back on the kit and try it with a very slow metronome setting (counting 16th notes all the way). Keep increasing the speed until you can approach the indicated tempo.

And here, ladies and germs, is the core, the essence, of *Kill 'Em All* (from a drumming standpoint, at least).

"Hit the Lights" Intro from *Kill 'Em All*

TRACK 38

With slight variations in tempo, fills, and the placement of cymbal crashes, Lars made this aggressive beat the cornerstone of "Hit the Lights," "Motorbreath," "Whiplash," "Phantom Lord," and "Metal Militia." He used it for intros, verses, pre-choruses, and choruses, as well as instrumental interludes. And to ratchet up the intensity a bit, he would simply throw more triplets on the fire during the guitar solos. Burn, baby, burn!

"Hit the Lights" Guitar Solo from *Kill 'Em All*

TRACK 39

Though bass drum triplets appear less frequently on subsequent albums, there are still some excellent examples on *Ride the Lightning, Master of Puppets,* and *. . . And Justice for All.* Just for fun (he said sadistically), here's one in 7/4 time. Remember, 7/4 is just like one 4/4 measure plus one 3/4 measure. Or one 3/4 measure plus one 4/4 measure—but who's counting? Hopefully, you are—always!

"Blackened" Second Verse from . . . *And Justice for All*

Moderately fast Rock ♩ = 182

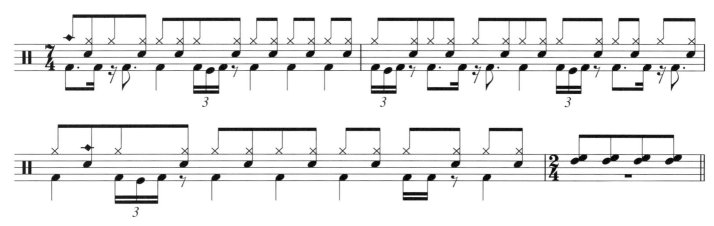

And here's one with a cool little floor tom ride pattern.

"Phantom Lord" Guitar Solo from *Kill 'Em All*

Moderate Rock ♩ = 108

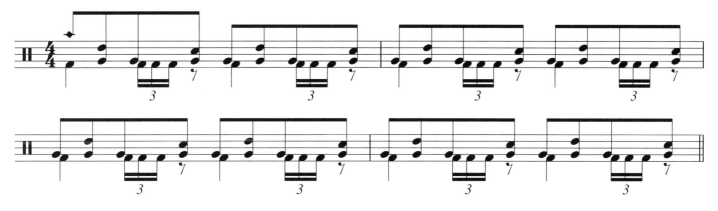

Well, so much for single bass triplets. As I trust you did with the 16th note pairs earlier in this chapter, go back through these examples and play the triplets with your weaker foot. This will probably feel very awkward at first, but do your best. Keep in mind that *solid* is always more important than *fast* when you're learning something new. After you've spent a few days getting comfortable with that, continue on to the next chapter.

CHAPTER 7

The Thunder Down Under—Further Adventures in Double Bass Drum Technique

No doubt, one of the things that first drew you to Metallica's music was Lars' prodigious double bass drum playing. So in the next few chapters, we'll be delving in detail into the double-barreled, wall-shaking, subwoofer-exploding power in the lower end of the kit.

A barrage of 16th notes played between two bass drums has long been associated with hard rock and metal drumming. But did you know that as far back as the 1940s, some drummers of the swing/big band era were experimenting with this technique? One such example was the late, great Louie Bellson who appeared in numerous promotional photographs behind his double bass drum kit.

However, rapid fire bass drum 16th notes in single-stroke roll fashion were used—at that time and in those musical styles—by only a few drummers and only during flashy featured solos. The heaviness of the sound was not considered appropriate for the percussive accompaniment to a song or tune. It wasn't until the 1960s—when advancements in technology paved the way for the more powerful amplification of vocals, guitars, keyboards and other instruments—that drummers began to unleash the possibilities of two bass drums within the body of a song.

And Lars is certainly one of the great ones. Not only is he a technical wizard, displaying incredible athleticism and dexterity, but he is also a consumate musician, allowing the various elements of a song (vocals, guitar or bass parts) to dictate when and how to make appropriate use of the "thunder down under." So practice the following examples. Master each version of Lars' double bass drum grooves, and then go back and hear for yourself the choices that he has made for the various sections within each song. Technique is only musical in the hands of a true musician—one who really listens to what's going on around him or her.

Before we begin, there are a few things to keep in mind as you work on your double bass drum playing.

- *Rhythmic Precision.* Steady 16th notes should be just that—*steady!* Always use your metronome and count.

- *Consistent Dynamics.* Right and left bass drum notes should be played at equal volumes to achieve the full effect.

- *No Unintentional Flamming.* This is a personal foul and a 15-yard penalty from the line of scrimmage. Whether you are playing a cymbal ride/snare drum backbeat pattern or doing a snare or tom fill over those bass drum 16ths, avoid flamming between the hands and feet. Try to make the notes land precisely together.

- *Setup Option.* If you can't use a second bass drum for whatever reason, don't despair. There are many high-quality double pedals on the market that allow you to play with two beaters on one drum. Although two drums are generally preferable for optimal feel and sound, you can certainly develop your technique on one drum with the use of a double pedal.

First, to make sure that your bass drum 16th notes are solid by themselves, practice the following exercise repeatedly until you begin to achieve the power and flow you are after. Play the exercise as written (first measure twice, second measure twice, etc.), and then try playing each measure four times. Finally, for some serious endurance, play each measure eight times. Start slowly, and pay attention to the quality of your sound as you increase the speed.

TRACK 42

Now, on top of those newly-perfected bass drum 16ths (which Lars plays RLRL, etc.), play a simple quarter note ride pattern on the hi-hat and backbeats on the snare drum, as in the following example.

"Fade to Black" Outro from *Ride the Lightning*

Lars uses that groove for a while before switching to the following beat, which is essentially the same except for the quarter notes on the snare drum.

"Fade to Black" Outro from *Ride the Lightning*

Here's an interesting twist—essentially, reverse the backbeats by playing the snare drum on beats 1 and 3. Lars starts off the first chorus of "Leper Messiah" with a simple single bass drum groove before getting into this double bass phrase. After two bars of snare quarters, the *double stop* (two parts of the kit struck simultaneously) tom rhythm in the last two bars accents the guitar part.

"Leper Messiah" Chorus from *Master of Puppets*

Most often, Lars plays a quarter note ride pattern on the hi-hat or ride cymbal when rocking steadily on these bass drum 16ths. Be sure to experiment with various eighth note or even 16th note ride patterns as well, and try riding on a crash or China cymbal for a less distinct, trashier sound. Just be sure to protect your ears with earplugs and/or headphones.

And speaking of different ride patterns, the floor tom can also be effectively used with double bass.

"Trapped Under Ice" Bridge from *Ride the Lightning*

♩ = 160

Words and Music by James Hetfield, Lars Ulrich and Kirk Hammett
Copyright © 1984 Creeping Death Music (ASCAP)
International Copyright Secured   All Rights Reserved

For the aforementioned guitar solo, Lars moves into a double time feel in the hands over those bass drum 16ths.

"Trapped Under Ice" Guitar Solo from *Ride the Lightning*

TRACK 47

Double time feel ♩ = 160

Words and Music by James Hetfield, Lars Ulrich and Kirk Hammett
Copyright © 1984 Creeping Death Music (ASCAP)
International Copyright Secured   All Rights Reserved

Practice the last two examples separately before combining them into one continuous passage of music as they occur on the original recording.

For a darker and less cluttered sound, simply avoid a ride pattern of any kind. In this example, Lars plays the backbeats with tom 1/tom 2 double stops as he gradually builds the phrase into a double-time section.

"Master of Puppets" Vocal Interlude from *Master of Puppets*

Finally, here's one more curve to throw at you. Occasionally, the steady stream of bass drum 16ths can be paused or broken with great effect, as the following examples show.

"Leper Messiah" Bridge from *Master of Puppets*

"Cure" Interlude from *Load*

Keep thinking about and listening for new and inventive ways to use this technique. The more you explore and experiment, the more you will feel "at home" with and in control of your double bass drum setup.

CHAPTER 8

The Triple Double—Triplets with Two Bass Drums

Remember those single bass drum 16th note triplets from Chapter 6? Well, beginning with *Master of Puppets,* Lars began to play his bass drum triplets on two drums with a RLR foot pattern. As the original recordings demonstrate, this gave him more control, definition, and power, particularly at high speeds. Compare the "(Anesthesia)—Pulling Teeth" example earlier in the book to this one from "Eye of the Beholder."

"Eye of the Beholder" Intro from . . . *And Justice for All*

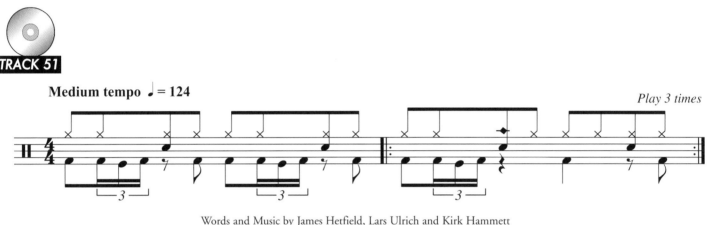

Words and Music by James Hetfield, Lars Ulrich and Kirk Hammett
Copyright © 1988 Creeping Death Music (ASCAP)
International Copyright Secured   All Rights Reserved

If you are still somewhat new to double bass drumming, this might feel uncomfortable at first, and it's most likely a simple balance issue. In single bass drum playing, we are generally accustomed to supporting our bodies by having one or both heels down on the pedals at all times. But when playing double bass drums, there are often times when both heels are up—either rebounding from, or in the act of, a pedal stroke—and we lose our sense of balance. To keep the rest of the body relaxed when this happens, it is important to sit up straight and focus your core, the trunk of your body, so that your center of gravity feels stable. You can practice this by sitting at the drumkit and lifting both heels slightly off the pedals. Find your center of gravity and adopt the position and posture with which you feel most supported without the help of your heels pressing up from the ground. Memorize this position and how you feel in it. Try to reproduce it every time you sit at the kit.

Back to the music. Whereas Lars played this on the band's first album . . .

"No Remorse" Guitar Solo from *Kill 'Em All*

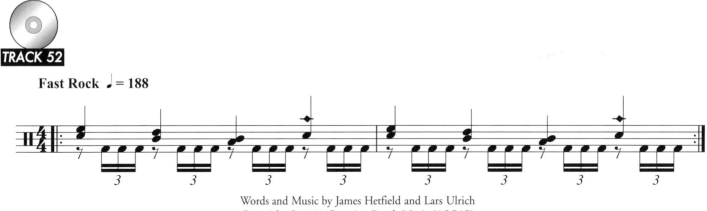

Words and Music by James Hetfield and Lars Ulrich
Copyright © 1983 Creeping Death Music (ASCAP)
International Copyright Secured   All Rights Reserved

. . . he played this on the third.

"Leper Messiah" Chorus from *Master of Puppets*

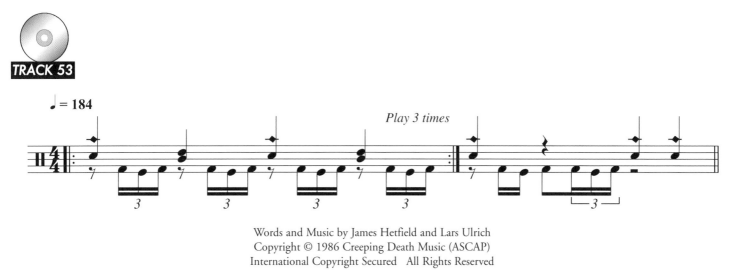

Words and Music by James Hetfield and Lars Ulrich
Copyright © 1986 Creeping Death Music (ASCAP)
International Copyright Secured   All Rights Reserved

Both examples have quarter notes in the hands that move around the drumset from one beat to the next, but in the later recording Lars goes for the greater "punch" of the double bass drum triplet.

And here's one more. Take another peek back in Chapter 6 at the first of the two examples from "Hit the Lights." Now, take a look at how Lars would later split the triplets like this.

"Dyers Eve" Intro from . . . *And Justice for All*

Words and Music by James Hetfield, Lars Ulrich and Kirk Hammett
Copyright © 1988 Creeping Death Music (ASCAP)
International Copyright Secured   All Rights Reserved

By the way, if you want to check out an awesome demonstration of double bass speed and power, listen to the entire original recording of "Dyers Eve." At 194 b.p.m., this track absolutely blisters!

CHAPTER 9

2 x 2—Four-Note Hand/Foot Combination Drills and 16th Notes on One and Two Bass Drums

So far, with only a few exceptions, we have seen bass drum 16th notes and 16th note triplets used as parts of grooves in which the hands play either a ride pattern with snare drum backbeats or tom double stops. But Lars also makes frequent use of four-note fills split between the hands and feet—two notes in the hands followed immediately by two in the feet. Although there is no official name for these commonly-played licks, we'll call them "2 x 2s" for ease of reference. In the first *Learn to Play Drums with Metallica* book, pages 43 and 44 briefly touch on this topic, but because these are such staples—such trademark licks—we'll investigate them further here.

First, let's deal with some single bass drum 16th note versions. Warm up with the following "2 x 2" exercise.

TRACK 55

Not always one for keeping it simple, Lars throws some flams into the mix.

"The Shortest Straw" Third Verse/Chorus from . . . *And Justice for All*

TRACK 56

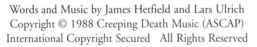

The hands can, of course, be moved around the kit from one drum to another like this—another great warm-up.

Words and Music by James Hetfield and Lars Ulrich
Copyright © 1988 Creeping Death Music (ASCAP)
International Copyright Secured   All Rights Reserved

TRACK 57

Take a look at this next example. For now, focus only on measures 7–12. Here, Lars alternates between measures of different time feels and a "2 x 2" fill. Practice these six bars thoroughly first.

"Ride the Lightning" Second Chorus from *Ride the Lightning*

TRACK 58

As you have no doubt noticed, the first of those six measures is in a double-time feel, the third measure is in straight time, and the fifth measure is in a half-time feel. Now, let's "zoom out" to look at the entire example and catch a glimpse of Lars' true brilliance—not in his power or speed but in his desire to play for the song. After the second chorus, the song goes into a double time feel section with the lyric "Someone help me. Oh, please God help me! They're trying to take it all away. I don't want to die." (This is precisely where our example starts.) The next major section of the song is the guitar solo, which has a half time feel. But instead of abruptly switching gears from a double time feel to a half time feel, Lars created this six-bar phrase in the middle to provide a smooth transition. Brilliant—and extremely musical!

Always think about the bigger musical picture. Yes, it's impressive to play loud and fast, but even that becomes dull for the listener if it doesn't make musical sense in the context of the song or if there is no variety. The music should always come first. Now, with all that in mind, go back and work on the entire example. And while you're at it, listen to the original recording to hear for yourself how that transition works.

Of course, all of the exercises and examples in the previous section can be played with two bass drums by playing the four-note grouping as follows: right hand/left hand/right foot/left foot. If you use a left-handed setup, try: left hand/right hand/left foot/right foot. With rare exceptions, though, the 16th note "2 x 2s" are played with a single bass drum. In contrast, for the 16th note triplet version, they're generally played with two bass drums. Here are some warm-up exercises to get you started.

TRACK 59

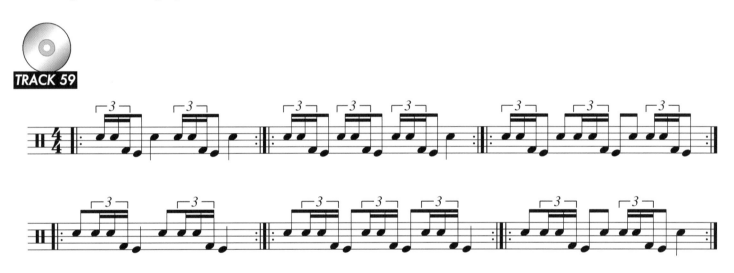

In "Disposable Heroes," Lars uses a "2 x 2" lick as a recurring theme tied to the lyric "Back to the front," as in this section just before the second verse.

"Disposable Heroes" Chorus from *Master of Puppets*

Words and Music by James Hetfield, Lars Ulrich and Kirk Hammett
Copyright © 1986 Creeping Death Music (ASCAP)
International Copyright Secured   All Rights Reserved

This idea of recurring themes, or *motifs,* attached to specific lyrics in contemporary songs can be traced back to the use of musical ideas representing specific characters or concepts in classical music. Just one more bit of proof that music is music, and no matter how different the styles may be, much of the language is shared. Listen to all kinds of music, and you will have more to bring to the table to make your brand of metal drumming that much more unique and interesting.

Here's a great little lick from the "Black Album." Don't freak out about the 32nd notes—the tempo is slow to mid-tempo meaty rock. The bass drum 32nd note triplets in the third measure are on the "a" of 1 and the "a" of 3, so the bass drum part in the first beat is counted, "1–e–and–a–trip–let" with the "a–trip–let" fitting into the last 16th note of the beat. The really cool part here, though, is the fill in the fourth measure. If you find it tricky to read, count, and/or play at first, listen to the demonstration track on the CD and count along (in 16ths). Stay with it. This lick and its many possible variations will surely be one that you'll stick in your back pocket; it will become one of your favorites. To hear The Master play it, check out the guitar solo after the second Chorus on "The God That Failed." Here are the first five measures from that solo.

"The God That Failed" Guitar Solo from *Metallica*

TRACK 61

Slow Rock ♩ = 76

Words and Music by James Hetfield and Lars Ulrich
Copyright © 1991 Creeping Death Music (ASCAP)
International Copyright Secured   All Rights Reserved

This next example, which comes from the final section of "Ride the Lightning," has two versions of the triplet "2 x 2." The first one is in measure 4—a 16th note triplet with snare/tom 1/bass drum 1/bass drum 2 starting on the downbeat. In the second (measure 6), the "2 x 2s" are played faster and somewhat squeezed together. Rhythmically, they are not played or counted as 16th note triplets; rather they are played like *four-stroke ruffs* (a basic snare drum rudiment). In other words, the main, or *principal* notes (the bass drum 2 eighth notes that are of normal print size) should land precisely in rhythm: "1–and–2–and–3–and–4". But the groups of three grace notes, (tom 3/tom 2/bass drum 1) that precede each principal (bass drum 2) eighth note are to be played very tightly together immediately before the principal note. Check out the CD track if this doesn't become clear to you after working at it for a few minutes.

By the way, If your setup does not have a third mounted ("rack") tom, substitute the floor tom for tom 3.

"Ride the Lightning" Coda from *Ride the Lightning*

TRACK 62

Moderate Rock ♩ = 150

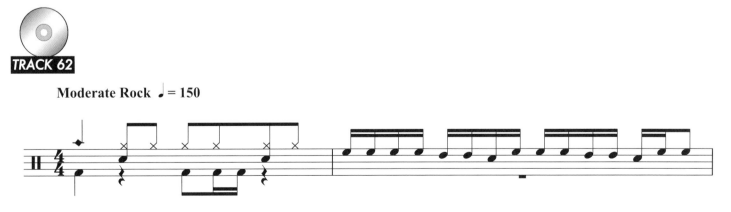

Words and Music by James Hetfield, Lars Ulrich, Cliff Burton and Dave Mustaine
Copyright © 1984 Creeping Death Music (ASCAP)
International Copyright Secured   All Rights Reserved

You should get in the habit of working written parts out by counting and practicing diligently instead of picking them up by listening to a recording. It's certainly not "cheating" to listen to a CD, and it *is* important to develop your musical ears, but it is equally important to your overall development as a musician to improve your reading skills.

Another great example of the total command Lars achieved by the time . . . *And Justice for All* was released is the four bars leading into the guitar solo on "Blackened." Again, it's a solid mid-tempo track (128 b.p.m.), but his use of "2 x 2s" here is quite crafty.

"Blackened" Interlude/Guitar Solo from . . . *And Justice for All*

TRACK 63

Slow Rock ♩ = 128

Words and Music by James Hetfield, Lars Ulrich and Jason Newsted
Copyright © 1988 Creeping Death Music (ASCAP)
International Copyright Secured   All Rights Reserved

As you can see, the first two "2 x 2s" are 32nd note licks starting on the "and" of beat 4 in measure 2, and on beat 2 in the next measure. The tricky thing with these is that there is no strong ending point rhythmically. They don't really *land*; they are just suspended, in a sense, ending on the last 32nd note before beat 1 and before the "and" of beat 2, respectively.

Measure 4 is very interesting in that Lars plays three "2 x 2s" consecutively without pause. The rhythm in the first two beats of the measure is written as two 16th note *sextuplets* (two beats of six-note groupings). Since "2 x 2s" are a four-note pattern, the second (middle) one is actually split between the two sextuplets. These two beats are phrased as "**1**–trip-let–and–**trip**-let–2–trip-**let**–and–trip-let." This can be a little confusing, so try playing the rhythm (with an accent at the start of every four-note grouping) on the snare drum first to get the hang of it.

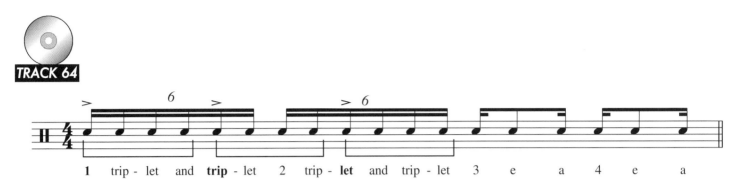

Once the rhythm is solid, return to the "Blackened" example and orchestrate it around the kit as written using the toms and bass drums.

Continue experimenting with this "2 x 2" idea and invent your own library of licks. There are so many possibilities, and some will lay more naturally than others in your hands and feet. These are the ones that will stay with you and become a permanent part of your drumming arsenal.

A Timely Tip from the Pros (At No Extra Charge)

If your drumming career is to be a long and fulfilling one (as we trust it will be), you will encounter a number of those precious and endearing moments of sheer terror and panic when your gear suddenly decides to take a vacation. In the style of the music being discussed here, it will undoubtedly be your bass drum double pedal/second pedal that goes south on you. And in that character-building eventuality, it's comforting to know that you *do* have an option— a technique to keep those "2 x 2" licks alive and in your show (provided you have spent some time practicing them). The solution is simply to replace the first of the two bass drum notes with a floor tom note. Genius, pure genius!!

The floor tom is not, of course, as deep or powerful as the kick drum. And while this would technically no longer be a "2 x 2" lick, the intended effect will still come across. Classic rock drummers, such as the immortal John Bonham of Led Zeppelin, made brilliant use of licks such as these on many famous tracks. Now, since you don't know which bass drum beater or pedal might decide to leave you high and dry, practice the following exercises using either the right or the left foot for the bass drum note.

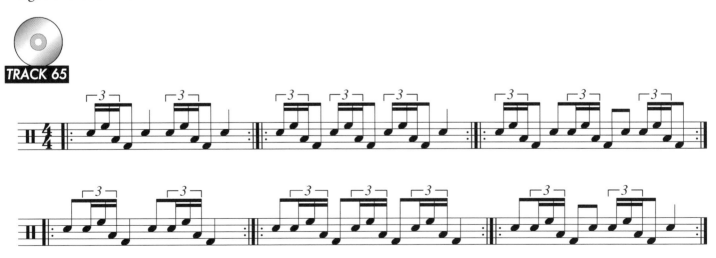

CHAPTER 10

All Within My Feet—Total Command of Double Bass Drums

Now that you have thoroughly practiced the double bass drum concepts in Chapters 7 through 9, it's time to put several of them together into a single musical passage. In order to freely move in and out from one technique to another without disrupting the time flow, you must have each individual groove, fill, and lick mastered at many different tempi. If one or two of them still take a bit of an effort to play smoothly, spend a few practice sessions now to nail those down before attempting to play the examples in this chapter.

This first example is a six-bar phrase—four measures of quarter notes in the hands with double bass drum triplets on the upbeats ("ands") followed by two measures of double bass drum 16ths on beats 1 and 3.

To practice this, break it up and work on just the first four bars to start. Play only the hands parts along with the metronome for a few minutes until that flows consistently. Next, of course, add the bass drum triplets. Gradually increase the speed up to (if not past) 136 b.p.m., the tempo on the original recording. Now, work on just the last two bars. Once both patterns are totally smooth and (relatively) effortless, slow the tempo back down and play the whole phrase. Make sure that the transition from measures 4 to 5 is fluid. Gradually push the tempo, and you've got it.

"Leper Messiah" Chorus from *Master of Puppets*

What makes this next one somewhat challenging—aside from the insanely fast tempo—is that the double bass groove does not have a traditional cymbal/snare pattern in the hands. Instead, the toms start on the "and" of 1 with a punctuated double stop rhythm. Again, split this one up to work on each groove separately before trying to join them together.

"Damage, Inc." Intro from *Master of Puppets*

Words and Music by James Hetfield, Lars Ulrich, Kirk Hammett and Cliff Burton
Copyright © 1986 Creeping Death Music (ASCAP)
International Copyright Secured   All Rights Reserved

Thus far, we've encountered only one technique/groove switch in each example, but this next one incorporates a floor tom ride pattern that instantly morphs (on beat 4 of the fourth measure) into a deceptively tricky double bass drum 16ths groove before making another sudden switch to a bass pairs beat and ending with a two-measure fill into the chorus/outro. Wow!

Watch out for the transition from the fourth bar to the fifth in this example. It is quite a challenge to "turn the corner" smoothly.

"Cure" Interlude from *Load*

Moderate Rock ♩ = 120

Here's a practice suggestion: After drilling measures 1 and 5 to perfection, put imaginary repeat signs around bars 4 and 5. Loop these two measures until you can play them in your sleep. Now, go back and try to play the first eight-bar phrase in its entirety. Use the imaginary repeat sign trick for bars 8 to 9 as well. Practicing this way takes a lot of discipline but, again, the payoff in results is huge!

Here's one that ought to keep you busy and entertained for a while. In the verse and chorus of "Blackened," Lars goes from a simple single bass drum pattern in 6/4 to a pattern with mixed single bass pairs and double bass triplets in 7/4 to some double bass 16ths patterns in straight time *and* double time. He even manages to throw in a few of those "2 x 2" hands/feet triplets for good measure. Now, that's Total Command, my friend. And, not for nothin', but . . . the tempo's 182!! Start off slowly, and work on one section at a time before putting them together. Have fun with this one—it's a blast once you get it!

"Blackened" Verse/Chorus from . . . *And Justice for All*

Moderately fast Rock ♩ = 182

*2nd time play crash on beat 4.

*2nd time play crash on beat 4.

2nd time substitute Fill 1

2nd time substitute Drum Fig. 1

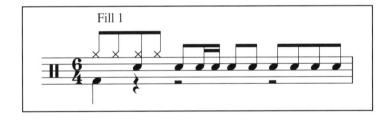

Fill 1

Drum Fig. 1

Words and Music by James Hetfield, Lars Ulrich and Jason Newsted
Copyright © 1988 Creeping Death Music (ASCAP)
International Copyright Secured   All Rights Reserved

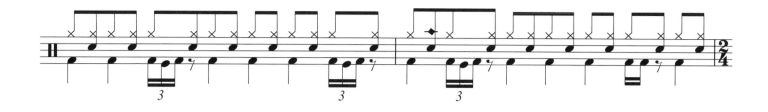

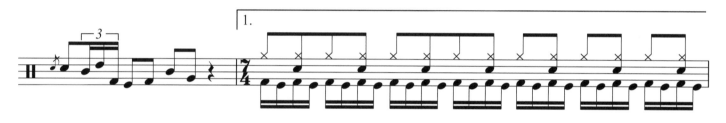

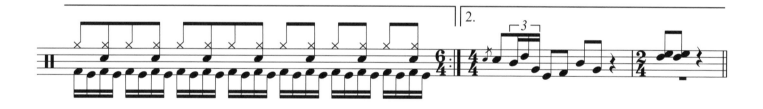

Here's one more for the road—and it's a beauty, my friends! Of all of the amazingly challenging drum tracks in Metallica's discography, "Dyer's Eve" stands out as an exceptionally fast, difficult, and varied showcase of double bass drum mastery. To get an idea of this double kick tour de force, check out what Lars plays during the guitar solo. Turn off the cell phone, pack some Gatorade and granola bars, and tell your friends and family that you'll see them in a week or two. Good luck.

"Dyers Eve" Guitar Solo from . . . *And Justice for All*

TRACK 70

Fast Rock ♩ = 194

CHAPTER 11

The Fill That Should Not Be—Flam and Double Bass Licks and Hands-Only Fills

As we've seen with Lars, every great drummer has his own unique "library of grooves"—those much-loved and oft-used beats and time feels that serve as the basis for the majority of a player's work. Likewise, most players have a "trick bag" of killer fills or licks. You know—the ones that just jump off the recording and grab your attention instantly, the ones that seem to come out of nowhere and make your jaw drop or get you air-drumming wildly.

Although Lars knows full well his primary responsibility of laying down a solid groove for the band, he does add in some mind-blowing fills. Often, he will use combinations of snare drum flams and bass drum triplets to knock our socks off and remind us that he can do far more than just play time—as long as it makes musical sense. Here are a few of this author's favorites.

First, take a look a few pages back at the fill into the guitar solo from "Blackened" in Chapter 9. The fill actually begins three measures before the solo, but rather than predictably playing time right up until the last bar, Lars builds the intensity by throwing in little pieces of fill (the 32nd note "2 x 2" licks) and then gives us the knockout punch with the sextuplet "2 x 2s." When practicing this fill, take care not to rush the last measure. It is very easy to become excited and barrel through it, and this can actually weaken the effect. Relax. Punch it out, but follow the metronome and stay in control of the time. Give this slamming lick its due.

This next "2 x 2" fill comes in a variety of flavors: single bass, double bass, snare, toms. One of the most common versions for Lars is this one from *Metallica*.

"The God That Failed" Guitar Solo from *Metallica*

TRACK 71

These eight measures provide an excellent loop on which to groove for days! And when you've mastered that, you can take it one step further by playing "2 x 4s" (with a nod to the tune on *Load*) by using a six-note pattern (snare/snare/bass drum 1/bass drum 2/bass drum 1/bass drum 2) instead of the usual four-note pattern (snare/snare/bass drum 1/bass drum 2).

Look at the example below, and this should begin to make sense. The fill bar is counted "**1**–**and**–trip-let–**2**–trip-let–**and**–**3**-trip-let–**and**–trip-let–**4**." It's a very cool variation, and the four-bar phrase again provides a smooth, natural exercise loop if you keep repeating it.

"Battery" Interlude from *Master of Puppets*

TRACK 72

Alright, let's go back to the early days for this next one. It's one of those single bass drum triplet specials that we all know and love. The fill starts on the "a" of beat 3 with a bass drum 32nd note triplet and a snare flam on beat 4. Take this very slowly, and try to count it out.

"Phantom Lord" Interlude from *Kill 'Em All*

TRACK 73

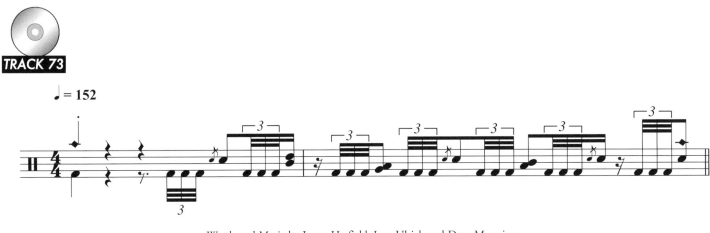

If you are finding it a little tricky to figure out the 32nd note triplets, you're not alone, and there is a relatively simple solution. By doubling the value of every note, you can write the fill this way just to get the feel of it.

Essentially, you cut the speed of the fill in half by rewriting the 32nd notes as 16ths, the 16ths as eighths, the eighths as quarters, and the quarters as half notes. Of course, since you doubled all of the note values (lengths), you now must play the lick at twice the original tempo (304 b.p.m.) to match the sound and speed of Lars' original idea. Pretty wicked, huh?!

But just so that you don't get the impression that a fill must use double bass drums and flams to come across powerfully on a recording. . . .

"Of Wolf and Man" Chorus from *Metallica*

Moderate Rock ♩ = 116

Words and Music by James Hetfield, Lars Ulrich and Kirk Hammett
Copyright © 1991 Creeping Death Music (ASCAP)
International Copyright Secured   All Rights Reserved

No big deal, right? It's just 16th notes with a few 32nd notes thrown in. Yes, but Lars plays it so solidly, so smoothly, and with so much confidence that you *believe* that fill! It's just right. Try this exercise to work on your single-stroke rolls.

TRACK 75

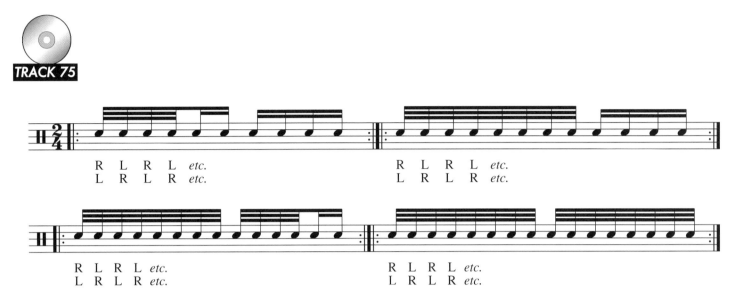

If you have a practice pad, start on that so you can clearly hear both the metronome and each note that you play. Strive for machine-like timing perfection and smooth dynamic evenness. Practice at several different tempos and volumes. Once you gain command of the exercise on the pad, work it out on the snare drum. Make sure that you can still hear the metronome (through headphones, perhaps). Next, try moving the exercise around the toms. And, of course, you can practice it with your feet as well. Knock yourself out!

CHAPTER 12

The House Lars Built—Growing and Maturing as a Drummer and a Musician

Now that we have thoroughly explored the technical side of drumming with Metallica, let's take a few minutes to look at the ways in which Lars has developed conceptually over the years—how he has learned to play more for the music than for himself.

Maturation is a good thing, especially in the case of making music. Over time, through study and experience, musicians gradually learn how to harness all of their collected knowledge, skill, and technical prowess to better serve the music they play. Drummers, particularly, tend to streamline their playing a bit—not to purposely tone it down or make it less energetic or interesting, but rather to create parts that just make more sense for the song and to the listener's ear. Parts that *support* more than *overpower*.

This natural evolution in any drummer's style is entirely evident in Lars' recording history with Metallica. And no matter which period in his (or the band's) development you prefer, it is important to have some understanding of how his drumming has changed over the years—how his musical "house" has been built up from its solid foundation and modified periodically in terms of design (creative growth) as well as stucture (technical development). Undoubtedly, if you continue "banging the skins" long enough, you will likely see some of these same changes over time in your own style and approach to the instrument and to music in general.

As we have seen in many of the examples in this book, the strength of the band's first release, *Kill 'Em All*, was its frenetic hyperdriving nature. The guys were young. The playing was raw, fast, and in your face. Beats tended to be static, one-measure phrases, but don't misunderstand this description—as Lars readily admits, the band really began to learn how to play in the year leading up to the release of *Ride the Lightning* and has continued to grow ever since.

Metallica's first four releases (*Kill*, *Lightning*, *Puppets*, and *Justice*) had many stylistic similarities. Most notable were the blazing tempos and incredible single and double bass drum work—the 16th and 32nd note triplets, the "2 x 2s", and the double bass drum rolls. As you can hear from the band's recordings, what changed drastically over the course of those albums was the enormous increase in technical facility and flexibility. Having become comfortable with many different variations of his early beats from *Kill*, Lars developed the ability to change things up "on the fly" at breakneck speeds.

"Welcome Home (Sanitarium)" Guitar Solo from *Master of Puppets*

TRACK 76

Double-time feel ♩ = 98

Words and Music by James Hetfield, Lars Ulrich and Kirk Hammett
Copyright © 1986 Creeping Death Music (ASCAP)
International Copyright Secured   All Rights Reserved

Aside from making the obvious technical improvements, though, Lars began to think and play in longer phrases. Instead of playing the same pattern in every measure, he began to play in two- and four-bar phrases. This allowed the drum parts to breathe and to have a more dynamic and natural circular flow. Next up is a perfect example.

"Creeping Death" Verse/Chorus from *Ride the Lightning*

TRACK 77

Fast Rock ♩ = 184

Words and Music by James Hetfield, Lars Ulrich, Cliff Burton and Kirk Hammett
Copyright © 1984 Creeping Death Music (ASCAP)
International Copyright Secured   All Rights Reserved

Did you notice that the Verse (measures 1–24) is played in two-bar phrases while the chorus (25–40) is based on four-bar phrases? Play this example a number of times until it becomes familiar and easy to play. Relax, and feel how the longer phrases make each section of music flow. Listen to the original recording as well to hear this in context.

How about thinking and playing in terms of an entire song section by taking a single musical idea—a groove, a fill, an accent pattern—and developing it, expanding it, over eight, 16, or more measures? Approaching a section this way can take the listener on a musical journey, and it is a great way to build interest and intensity.

"King Nothing" Bridge from *Load*

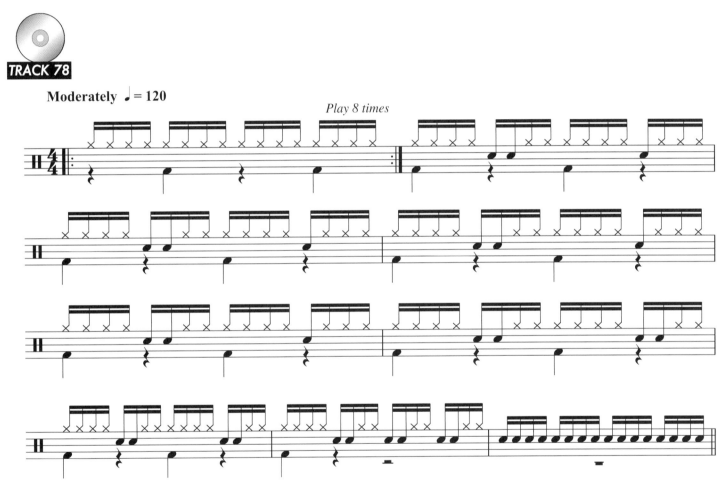

"The Thorn Within" Outro from *Load*

Moderate Rock ♩ = 116

Words and Music by James Hetfield, Lars Ulrich and Kirk Hammett
Copyright © 1996 Creeping Death Music (ASCAP)
International Copyright Secured   All Rights Reserved

Another way to grow as a drummer is to listen constantly to new music—by this, I mean music that is new *to you*. Check out other metal bands, of course, and learn from what their drummers have to say, but also listen to drummers in other styles. There's a great big world of music out there, and influences from those styles—rock 'n' roll, jazz, world beat, country, pop, reggae, you name it—can only serve to make your playing, your personal approach to metal drumming, that much more creative, interesting, and unique. And don't listen only to contemporary artists. Go back and delve into the music that came before.

And even if all of this study doesn't make you alter *how you play*, it might just change *what you play on*. It might lead you to explore a greater variety of sound sources on the kit. On the first five recordings, for instance, Lars' ride patterns were often quarter notes or eighth notes on either the *bow* (mid-section between the bell and the edge of the ride cymbal) on a steady closed hi-hat, or on a steady open and washy hi-hat. From *Load* on, Lars experimented with new sounds and feels much more frequently. From a riding pattern of 16th notes with *hi-hat slurs* (the quick opening and closing of the hi-hat cymbals for that "vacuum" effect) . . .

"Ronnie" Outro from *Load*

TRACK 80

Moderately slow Rock ♩ = 92

Words and Music by James Hetfield and Lars Ulrich
Copyright © 1996 Creeping Death Music (ASCAP)
International Copyright Secured   All Rights Reserved

. . . to quarter notes on the *bell* (the raised center dome) of the ride cymbal . . .

"Better Than You" Bridge from *ReLoad*

Moderately fast Rock ♩ = 160
Half-time feel

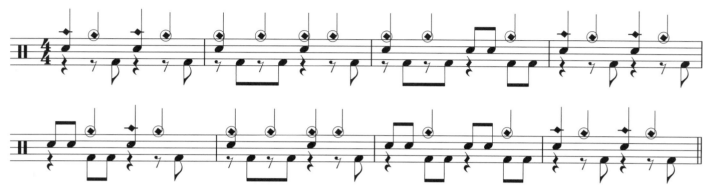

Words and Music by James Hetfield and Lars Ulrich
Copyright © 1997 Creeping Death Music (ASCAP)
International Copyright Secured   All Rights Reserved

. . . to a broken 16th note riding pattern on the snare drum . . .

"Where the Wild Things Are" Intro from *ReLoad*

Moderately slow Rock ♩ = 92

Words and Music by James Hetfield, Lars Ulrich and Jason Newsted
Copyright © 1997 Creeping Death Music (ASCAP)
International Copyright Secured   All Rights Reserved

. . . to the washy ride cymbal edge, snare drum with snares off, and splash cymbal on *St. Anger* (Metallica's last studio release), Lars has long sought to create completely new groove approaches for himself and for the band's music with simple changes in sound sources and ride patterns. And so should you!

CHAPTER 13

Welcome Home (Sanitarium)—Further Study

Congratulations! You made it. I trust that this has been a worthwhile adventure and an enjoyable ride. Or perhaps you're so fried now that you just might be in need of a sanitarium. Either way, take a well-deserved break. Treat yourself to a nice dinner and a night on the town. Maybe a weekend getaway. No matter how you choose to chill, I have a feeling that you'll be back for more. Soon enough, you'll be back behind those drums, thirsty for more knowledge and hungry just to play! Here are some suggestions for continuing down that road to metal drumming enlightenment.

First, if you aren't already in a band, find some musicians to play with so that you can put all of these newfound skills and concepts to good use. Take some private lessons. Buy some new CDs. If you are interested in *completely* absorbing Lars' style and technique, look into purchasing and working through the Metallica drum transcriptions. There is a volume for each of the band's recordings, and each book contains the complete drum and vocal parts for every song on that recording. All transcriptions come complete with drum notation keys and form indications, and provide you with the opportunity to work on your reading skills while learning to play the music you love.

Two outstanding examples for studying different sides to Lars' playing are "The God That Failed" from *Metallica* and "Disposable Heroes" from *Master of Puppets*. While "God" is a musical, creative, sweet, solid track with sextuplets, 32nd notes, and double bass drum flurries thrown into the mix, "Heroes" is a double kick showcase featuring half-time feel, double-time feel, "thunder down under" bass drum 16th notes, "2 x 2" licks, bass drum triplet figures, and mixed meters.

Between practicing sessions with the transcriptions and intense listening sessions with the original Metallica recordings, you will soon find yourself learning to play entire songs exactly the way he does . . . well, at least, we all have something to aim for!

Happy drumming!

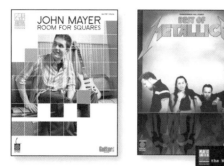

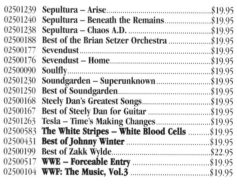

METALLICA

Visit Cherry Lane Online at
www.cherrylane.com

Prices, contents and availability subject to change without notice.

MATCHING FOLIOS

...AND JUSTICE FOR ALL
02506965	Play-It-Like-It-Is Guitar	$22.95
02506982	Play-It-Like-It-Is Bass	$19.95
02506856	Easy Guitar	$12.95
02503504	Drums	$18.95

GARAGE INC.
02500070	Play-It-Like-It-Is Guitar	$24.95
02500075	Play-It-Like-It-Is Bass	$24.95
02500076	Easy Guitar	$14.95
02500077	Drums	$18.95

KILL 'EM ALL
02507018	Play-It-Like-It-Is Guitar	$19.95
02507039	Play-It-Like-It-Is Bass	$19.95
02506860	Easy Guitar	$12.95
02503508	Play-It-Like-It-Is Drums	$18.95

LIVE: BINGE AND PURGE
02501232	Play-It-Like-It-Is Guitar	$19.95

LOAD
02501275	Play-It-Like-It-Is-Guitar	$24.95
02505919	Play-It-Like-It-Is-Bass	$19.95
02506881	Easy Guitar	$15.95
02503515	Drums	$18.95

MASTER OF PUPPETS
02507920	Play-It-Like-It-Is Guitar	$19.95
02506961	Play-It-Like-It-Is Bass	$19.95
02506859	Easy Guitar	$12.95
02503502	Drums	$18.95

METALLICA
02501195	Play-It-Like-It-Is Guitar	$22.95
02505911	Play-It-Like-It-Is Bass	$19.95
02506869	Easy Guitar	$14.95
02503509	Drums	$18.95

RE-LOAD
02501297	Play-It-Like-It-Is Guitar	$24.95
02505926	Play-It-Like-It-Is Bass	$21.95
02506887	Easy Guitar	$15.95
02503517	Drums	$18.95

RIDE THE LIGHTNING
02507019	Play-It-Like-It-Is Guitar	$19.95
02507040	Play-It-Like-It-Is Bass	$17.95
02506861	Easy Guitar	$12.95
02503507	Drums	$17.95

S&M HIGHLIGHTS
02500279	Play-It-Like-It-Is Guitar	$24.95
02500288	Play-It-Like-It-Is Bass	$19.95

COLLECTIONS

BEST OF METALLICA
02500424	Transcribed Full Scores	$24.95

BEST OF METALLICA
02502204	P/V/G	$17.95

5 OF THE BEST
02506210	Play-It-Like-It-Is Guitar – Vol. 1	$12.95
02506235	Play-It-Like-It-Is Guitar – Vol. 2	$12.95

LEGENDARY LICKS
AN INSIDE LOOK AT THE STYLES OF METALLICA
Book/CD Packs
02500181	Guitar 1983-1988	$22.95
02500182	Guitar 1988-1996	$22.95
02500180	Bass Legendary Licks	$19.95
02500172	Drum Legendary Licks	$19.95

LEGENDARY LICKS DVDS
A STEP-BY-STEP BREAKDOWN OF
METALLICA'S STYLES AND TECHNIQUES
02500479	Guitar 1983-1988	$24.95
02500480	Guitar 1988-1997	$24.95
02500481	Bass 1983-1988	$24.95
02500484	Bass 1988-1997	$24.95
02500482	Drums 1983-1988	$24.95
02500485	Drums 1988-1997	$24.95

RIFF BY RIFF
02506313	Guitar – Riff by Riff	$19.95

INSTRUCTION

METALLICA WITH EASY GUITAR
WITH LESSONS, VOLUME 1
02506877	Easy Recorded Versions	$14.95

METALLICA – EASY GUITAR
WITH LESSONS, VOLUME 2
02500419	Easy Guitar	$14.95

LEARN TO PLAY WITH METALLICA
Book/CD Packs
02500138	Guitar	$12.95
02500189	Bass	$12.95
02500190	Drums	$12.95

PLAYERS

THE ART OF KIRK HAMMETT
02506325	Guitar Transcriptions	$17.95

THE ART OF JAMES HETFIELD
02500016	Guitar Transcriptions	$17.95

REFERENCE

METALLICA – THE COMPLETE LYRICS
02500478	Lyrics	$19.95

CHERRY LANE
MUSIC COMPANY
6 East 32nd Street, New York, NY 10016

Quality in Printed Music

EXCLUSIVELY DISTRIBUTED BY

HAL•LEONARD®
CORPORATION
7777 W. BLUEMOUND RD. P.O. BOX 13819 MILWAUKEE, WI 53213